Praise for

A BLACK MAN'S POINT OF VIEW:
MIND, BODY, AND SOUL

"*A Black Man's Point of View: Mind Body and Soul* is a must-read for all, especially for young, coming-of-age men. It is a labor of love and a tribute to all those who came before us. It is a gripping, uplifting, and emotional read that will stay with you long after you turn the final page."

> —Bernadette Semple, Navy Commander (Ret.), United States Navy

"This essential, of-the-moment, wonderfully honest and frank must-read is far more than a memoir. Dr. Cooley's *A Black Man's Point of View* beautifully unfolds a universally relevant human experience that any American who is paying attention to the national crises affecting American life won't be able to put down. Dr. Cooley generously shares the usually not-fit-for-air details about growing up and becoming a Black leader in the face of usually unknowable struggles, challenges, and seemingly insurmountable obstacles, and he shows us how to learn from his—and our own—experiences. *A Black Man's Point of View* belongs on any shelf alongside Ta-Henisi Coates, Robyn Maynard, Rinaldo Walcott, and John Lewis, and, indeed, on the top of every nightstand."

> —Hon. Benjamin J. Mantell, Administrative Law Judge, City of New York; Queens County, NY, Assistant District Attorney 2003–2011; New York State Assistant Attorney General 2011–2013

"Dr. Cooley imparts some very important insights in his book. The stories give insights into what it is to be a Black man in today's America. James's journey has been longer and far more arduous than what he shares here, so he knows from what he speaks. His portion informs the reader of the credo by which he lives. This is what has guided him to become the brilliant and loving person he is.

"The other ten writers give slightly different perspectives on what it is to overcome and become successful Black men in their fields. This is a worthy and inspirational read for people of all races, genders, and ages."

—Sandy Dodson, Retired Pastor and Businessperson

"This . . . is a must-read! It provides invaluable information relative to knowledge and understanding experiences, encounters, lessons learned, and circumstances men of color face that help shape them to become the dynamic individuals they are today, as each of them fulfill their purpose of serving others to make the world a better place.

"I would advise individuals to purchase this book for themselves, family, friends, mentors/mentees (both youth and adults), and book clubs."

—Dr. Angela Seay, Chief Visionary Officer, D3 Health Fitness, LLC

"*A Black Man's Point of View: Mind, Body, and Soul,* is a highly worthwhile read, written by an incredible human being whose humble beginnings became the start of a journey to greatness.

"Author Dr. James Cooley is an African American who

received the venerable Presidential Legacy Lifetime Achievement Award (2023) and lives his life fully as husband, father, Veteran, businessman, author, motivational speaker, and humanitarian.

"In his groundbreaking book, Dr. Cooley reveals his incredible story of transcendence over prejudice and inequality by creating his own life to become one of opportunity, equality, and self-actualization. Though acknowledging that prejudice is oftentimes accompanied by hatred is a global phenomenon, Dr. Cooley believes—and conveys this belief by his own example—that there is the ability to transcend the hurts from the past towards advancement, healing, and enrichment for the future of our global community.

"Believing that 'all people are the same' regardless of race or color, Dr. Cooley aspires to

to help change our world with the philosophy 'Don't live according to how the world looks today, (but) live your life based on how it should be.'

"Reading Dr. James Cooley's incredible book also reminds us of the intrinsic, invisible human spirit residing from within, and its yearning to be loved and accepted for who and what we are and not by the color of our skin."

—Laurie Edwards-Tate, MS, President and Founder, At Your Home Familycare, Writer, Teacher, Think Local First Supporter; Director of the Board for Largest Hospital Healthcare District in California

"Empowering. What Dr. Cooley is sharing in this work is an authoritative reflection of his life and wisdom gained. He, along with his 'guest authors,' makes no apologies and lays no blame for history, both good and bad, and magnifies the need to have faith, love, and vision as we journey along our path through God's plan. *A Black Man's Point of View* reminds us to live intentionally with good purpose, surrounded by a 'chosen family' of people of good character, regardless of race, creed, or color. His message from a Black man to a Black man is to dispel labels, choose deliberately to see and accept God's gifts, and make choices to advance to a greater you, a greater us, and a greater nation and world. Dr. Cooley reminds all of us that we can change the world for the better through our actions, but you can't know where you are going if you don't understand where you have been. We all stand on the shoulders of those who went before us, and we owe it to them to advance, always advance. You own the power; wield it well."

—Quint Avenetti, CWO5 USMC (Ret.), Author of The Trail to Leadership: Securing America's Future One Boy at a Time; Veteran Mentor, Public Speaker, US Patent Holder, Corporate Executive

"A blueprint to overcoming and persevering through the challenges of a complex American society. The belief in God and the blessings that was bestowed among the writers really stood out in this book, which could be very inspirational for the religious communities. I was intrigued by the way the writers revealed how they overcame the effects of social and economic bias and a racist society. Very good read. Can't wait to read it again and again."

—Greg Mitchell, USMC (Ret.)

"This essential, of-the-moment, wonderfully honest and frank must-read is far more than a memoir. Dr. Cooley's *A Black Man's Point of View* beautifully unfolds a universally relevant human experience that any American who is paying attention to the national crises affecting American life won't be able to put down. Dr. Cooley generously shares the usually not-fit-for-air details about growing up and becoming a Black leader in the face of usually unknowable struggles, challenges, and seemingly insurmountable obstacles, and he shows us how to learn from his—and our own—experiences. *A Black Man's Point of View* belongs on any shelf alongside Ta-Henisi Coates, Robyn Maynard, Rinaldo Walcott, and John Lewis, and, indeed, on the top of every nightstand."

—Hon. Benjamin J. Mantell, Administrative Law Judge, City of
New York; Queens County, NY, Assistant District Attorney
2003–2011; New York State Assistant Attorney General
2011–2013

"In *A Black Man's Point of View*, Dr. Cooley transparently shares insights from his personal journey as man who happens to be Black. He shares an encouraging, uplifting, and honest message built on hope, faith, purpose, and a commitment to constantly moving forward despite obstacles, challenges, and setbacks that we all experience in our lives. Dr. Cooley's message is one that is vitally needed today. All readers will be encouraged and challenged to be and become their absolute best selves."

—Cedric X. Bryant, PhD, FACSM, President and Chief Science
Officer, American Council on Exercise

"Reading A *Black Man's Point of View*, I learned about the experiences and viewpoints of twelve men with a variety of backgrounds. While James Cooley and his eleven co-contributors grew up under different circumstances and had diverse careers, many had similar messages to share, such as the importance of the relationship between a child and parent and how being with your soul mate helps you reach your highest potential.

All readers will learn the essential traits of being a good man: keeping a positive attitude, demonstrating leadership, and showing compassion to others."

—James C. McMahon, PhD

"This book is powerful and anointed to touch lives, demonstrating God's most powerful love and sacrifice of His only begotten Son Jesus Christ! He paid for all our sins. God manifests his love, care, and grace. No man understands what is in every Black man. Only God almighty knows a Black man's heart!

"God's love is demonstrated through the training, coaching, and mentoring we all experience in times when we face challenges and difficulties. From the young, handsome Master James Cooley to Dr. James JC Cooley! You grasped God's purpose for your life in time!"

—Her Excellency Olivia Mirembe Musisi, Ambassador at Large of the Special Diplomatic Envoy to Southern and Eastern Africa Region, Liberland Diplomatic Liaison Officer for the Office of the Crown Prime Minister of the Queendom of Sheba

"As always, Dr. James JC Cooley, does not disappoint. His book *A Black Man's Point of View: Mind, Body, and Soul from the Voices of Black Men* drives home the point that each person's uniqueness makes them perfect for God's purpose. Dr. Cooley shares his most private life experiences as a Black male from childhood to the current day and incorporates universal wisdom that we all can learn from, regardless of race, color, gender, or age. He is a firm believer that life's individual destinations help us to reach our divine destiny. This books uplifts, motivates, and shines a light on the challenges that Black men face and continue to overcome. Each chapter is short and meaningful with an inspirational nugget for all to enjoy. The heartfelt stories from the ten contributing Black male authors bring a distinctive perspective to the book and are a definite bonus. If you feel or have even the slightest inkling that God has a plan for your life, then reading this book will help solidify your calling and put you on His path. It is a must-read for everyone, especially Black men."

—Bernadette Meeks, SMSgt, USAFR (Ret.)

"The *Souls of Black Folk* is a book written by Dr. W. E. B. Du Bois, published in 1903. The book is a collection of essays that explore the experiences and struggles of Black Americans in the United States at the turn of the twentieth century and identify what is needed to attain success and equality.

"Fast forward to 120 years later: *A Black Man's Point of View: Mind, Body, and Soul*, written by Dr. James Cooley, is published in 2023. His book is also a collection of essays that provide real-world experiences, life lessons, and a road map to get to the promised land of success.

"Dr. Cooley's writing is both vivid and powerful. He paints a vivid picture of the harsh realities of life that inspired and propelled him and the other authors to success and not failure.

"The book in many ways is a dichotomy in that it does an excellent job of exploring the themes of family, love, loyalty, and faith in the faith of adversity; while, on one hand, their stories of individual struggles and how to successfully navigate impediments in life are heart-wrenching and seemingly daunting. . . . It is a powerful reminder of the strength of the human spirit, bravery, tenacity, sacrifice, and courage of Black men—men who have traversed this journey called life in the face of unimaginable hardship and emerged victorious.

"Overall, *A Black Man's Point of View: Mind, Body, and Soul* is a must-read for all, especially for young, coming-of-age men.

It is a labor of love and a tribute to all those who came before us. It is a gripping, uplifting, and emotional read that will stay with you long after you turn the final page."

—Bernadette Semple, Navy Commander (Ret.), United States Navy

"'Do not let life happen to you, you should be the one to make it happen.' This is one of the gems one can expect by reading this book. Dr. Cooley provides us with fresh, light, and insightful, to-the-point knowledge that will help any man to find focus, perspective, motivation, determination, and creativity. By exploring the collective generational experience gathered over the years by himself and peers, the reader gets to realize, remember, and learn that when facing life's greatest challenges, there are magnificently powerful and efficient tools and solutions to tackle them. This book will provide any Black man the means to face the giant in his life. It is wonderful reading for the younger generation looking to get ahead mentally and build strength. It is a poignant reminder for older readers that they are not alone, that they have fellow men that made it [and] thrive and that they can achieve it too. Dr. Cooley, thanks for paying it forward and sharing with us your relevant insights."

—The Most Honorable Imperial Crown Vizier, Prime Minister of Sheba, Governor of Governors of Her Imperial Majesty, His Royal Highness, Prince Fritz Gerald Zephir

A BLACK MAN'S POINT OF VIEW

Mind, Body, and Soul

DR. JAMES JC COOLEY

TABLE OF CONTENTS

PREFACE

AS I SIT BACK and reminisce about my life over the last six decades and think about the trials and tribulations that took me on this journey, I believe that it has not been all about me but about what God's plans were for me.

I have been successful and unsuccessful along this journey, but I believe that success outweighs failures. This book is not meant to be self-obsessed, but it does address the young boy and young man I was and the man I am today. Regardless of where you start, that is not your final destiny. I believe we will experience several destinations along the way to realize what God's true purpose is for us.

I discuss what's in the heart of this Black man, but that only pertains to me. We must truly look at previous generations that have led us to where we are today and see that no man and no woman is an island, but it starts from knowing where you came from.

I wrote this book to let readers know that many failures will come before success follows. Understanding our forefathers' sacrifices helps us discover who we are. *The Black Man's Point of View* is all about my experiences and thoughts as it happened in my lifetime, and it's my answer to the question, "What's in the heart of this Black man?"

I hope you enjoy reading this book and the different scenarios, ideas, and compilations that may help you understand a Black man. Regardless of race, creed, or color, it is all about knowing who you are.

Thank you.

—Dr. James JC Cooley

Michael R. Mantell, PhD

WHEN MY HERALDED AND nationally acclaimed friend, Dr. James JC Cooley, asked me to write the foreword to this very personal account of the guiding principles of his life—indeed, of the lives of all humanity—I was admittedly astounded. Me? Seriously?

But that's what Dr. Cooley does in his daily life. He astonishes, amazes, and electrifies us all. That talent, his God-given inner resource, is what is in the heart of this powerfully stirring gentleman. He uplifts me, and for that, I am forever grateful. I share his principles with my psychological education coaching clients and in my presentations, and his impact deservedly spreads plentifully.

I was born in Newark, New Jersey. I grew up in the middle of the 1967 riots in my hometown and watched my father's shoe stores eventually burn. I later learned that the leaders initially told people in the streets to leave my dad's stores alone since what was in my father's heart led him to take care of people in the neighborhoods, anchored in his "love, compassion, reason, and the vision to love . . . regardless of race, religion, creed, or color." And that connection, I believe, is what God sees that brings Dr. Cooley and I together—his deeply felt emotions and his earned wisdom that fill the pages of this inspirational work, the words that fill his heart, the words that need to fill the world!

From the extreme dangers living first in Chattanooga, Tennessee, to the love he felt in Graham, Alabama, despite the extraordinary lack of modern conveniences, what grew in JC was a sensitivity for others, a passionate connection to the Lord, and a genuine appreciation that the trials and tribulations that shaped him as a person happened *for* his benefit. These are the seeds that bestow him with his formidable ability to positively influence and uplift us all today, in every corner of our globe, to courageously bring goodness to the planet . . . with love of God, family, people, and the love for everything and everybody.

As James pulls back the curtain to reveal his two failed marriages and two near-death experiences, among other difficulties, the reader wonders how anyone can grow through these weighty adversities and emerge with such potent vision and strength. Reading this book provides attention-grabbing insights and persuasive perspective shifts we can all use as we face the challenges placed in our paths.

I'm filled with so many life lessons found in this volume, but one stands out: "Never burn or destroy the bridge. It will be almost impossible to reconnect or get back on the same road, and those dreams from the ultimate love story can be hard to find once they're lost."

His love, devotion, and frank reliance on his wife, his executive producer, his chosen and trusted soulmate, Dr. Michelle, exemplifies what comes from his heart. He is not a bridge burner; he is a bridge builder, always resiliently moving forward, never backward. Never.

This book is a map to a greater life from the heart of a man who has experienced the sandpapering of life's misfortunes and harsh conditions. He shows us how beliefs, convictions, and a healthy mentality can help propel a life worth living, a life worth sharing, and a life worth respecting.

The ten co-contributors who join Dr. Cooley in these momentous pages provide the seasoning to the main course—the life lessons of unconditionally accepting God's plan for one's life through a lens of love. The diversity promoted here—internal, external, and worldwide—is what the world needs now more than ever. This book promises to be the spark that ignites and opens eyes and hearts, moves the needle in the direction of identifying our collective, unified human purpose—embracing and respecting the healthy changes that come *for* us in our society—and keeps our GPS systems focused on the good that will surely come tomorrow. My GPS system—gratitude, positivity, and sensitivity—is, I know, shared by Dr. Cooley.

What an honor and distinction for me to write this foreword. It will only be matched—indeed, surpassed—by the medallion that readers will proudly and respectfully wear upon digesting and living the teachings found inside the heart of this unrivaled and compelling author.

—Michael R. Mantell, PhD

THIS BOOK IS DEDICATED to the women with the most influence in my upbringing and in shaping the person I am today. Grandma, you guided me through the earliest years of my life. I will always remember the love, attention, and most importantly, the many words of wisdom you instilled in my heart and mind—all people are good people until they show you otherwise. Grandma, I miss you so much. You are my inspiration for everything that I do on this Earth.

Mama, I always think about you and the love you gave me when I felt like I was out of place in life. Thanks for having the faith and confidence to choose me and Jerry to live in Alabama with Uncle Robert and Aunt Geneva. They instilled in me values, confidence, and a solid work ethic. I miss you, Mama. You will always be there with every thought and every second that I have left on this Earth. I love you, Mama.

I want to thank my youngest sister Gayla (Gayle) Holloway Suttles who is no longer with us. However, you are with me every day. I can't believe that I cannot pick up the phone and call you to tell you what is on my mind and in my heart. You were my inspiration and told me I could do anything in life. I believe that my little sister helped shape the person I am today because she saw things and believed in me when no one else in the family did. I miss you so much. I love you so much. It is just so hard to imagine life without talking to you when there are challenges or trials and tribulations in my heart. I love you, Sis. I miss you, Sis. May God bless us on Heaven and Earth. We will one day see each other again. Love you.

—Dr. James JC Cooley

WHAT'S IN THE HEART OF THIS BLACK MAN

INITIALLY, I WAS ASKED to be one of sixteen coauthors collaborating to write a book titled *The Heart of a Black Man.*

I was to write one chapter consisting of one thousand words or less. I agreed to do this; however, as I was writing the requested chapter, I realized that I do not know what's in the heart of every Black man, but what I do know is what's in the heart of this Black man. In this book, my goal is to expand on my thoughts, beliefs, and opinions and share what helped create the man and person I am today. This is truly my character, and I truly stand by my convictions today.

I understand that we can only truly write about what we believe to be our truth. However, as we grow and experience new things, life's initial truths may change as we change. What's most important is God's plan for our lives. One thing we need to understand is that change is inevitable. It is going to happen.

I intend to convey my honest thoughts without bias and my true feelings when it comes to needs and wants. Previous generations taught me lessons and led me to write about what's in the heart of this Black man. I hope that readers are not offended by the things I believe to be true in my heart. I believe everyone has a looking glass, and this glass is just like looking in the mirror; the mirror reflects true reality of how things are only to the person looking in it. Our perceptions shape and determine our true realities and beliefs.

I believe we all have the same common birthrights regardless of what our beliefs might be—confidence, courage, hope, belief, and most importantly faith. However, there is another birthright that is uncommon to anyone else other than you. I call this your *secret sauce*. This birthright guides you to your purpose in life

Let me provide an example. In many of my speeches, I explain that as we are born, as we learn, and as we grow, we are all presented with our own personal key. This key is not a physical object, but it is a metaphorical key that is a personal gift from God to everybody born in His kingdom. I believe we may be presented with many doors, but this key only fits the door that God chose for you for your purpose. Therefore, we must be careful which door we stick the key in because it will dissolve. My point is that it requires knowledge and understanding to unlock God's purpose for us. This requires us to be patient, regardless of the trials and tribulations we will face in several destinations in life.

As I mentioned before, vison and understanding provide the key to unlocking several generational curses that might have been passed down to us. I had to receive and accept God to grasp His purpose for my life, regardless of what happened in the past or previous generations. I had to truly understand that God chose me to deliver a purpose to others.

I believe no one truly understands what's in the heart of every Black man. I would like to say what's in the heart of any man regardless of race, creed, and color, but I can only truly share what's in the heart of *this* Black man. I hope you enjoy reading my book.

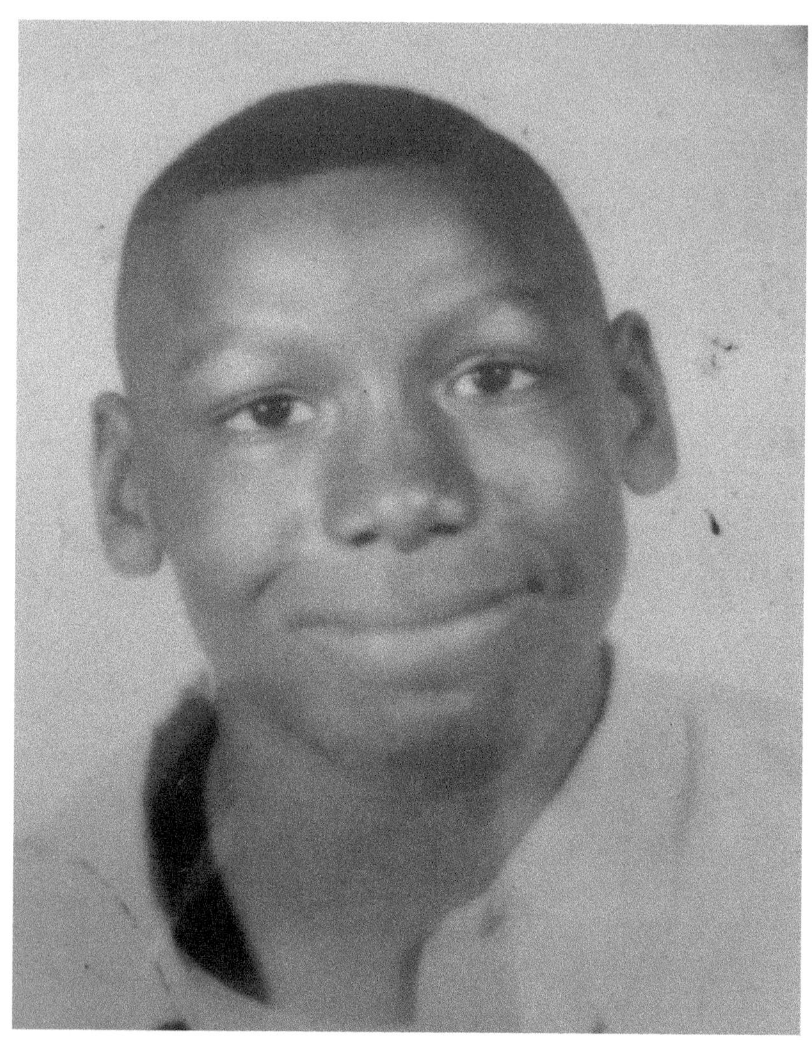

CHAPTER ONE

THE BEGINNING

WE MUST UNDERSTAND THE beginning to understand our destiny. I was born in Chattanooga, Tennessee, the seventh child of my wonderful mother, who had ten children by six different fathers but was never married.

For future chapters to make sense, I must start with my first published writing, *My Path.*

I grew up in one of the most dangerous housing project areas in Chattanooga. In 1965, my mother was unable to take care of all ten children. She chose to send my brother Jerry (seven years old) and me (six years old) to Graham, Alabama, to live with my Uncle Robert and Aunt Geneva Stephens. I remember knowing, even as a young child living in Chattanooga, that it was very difficult for my mother to feed all of us kids, but we did have modern accommodations—electricity, indoor plumbing, bathrooms, a stove, heat, and a fridge. My new accommodations in Alabama, however, were vastly different. We had no modern electricity, no indoor plumbing, no bathrooms, no stove, no heat, no fridge. Instead, we had a well with a rope and pulley, an outhouse in the pasture for bathroom service, and a small smokehouse to preserve our food, along with chickens, a few pigs, and cows, and—most importantly—a mule to help us gather firewood and haul other things.

My point is that, despite the lack of modern conveniences, I felt extremely rich because the biggest thing I had in Alabama was *love.* That is where I gained my knowledge, understanding, and core values (my foundation) that I live by today. I believe that being exposed to love, honesty, and trust gives us the building blocks that create our character.

I lived with my aunt and uncle for five and a half years before returning to Chattanooga to reunite with my mother and siblings. Upon returning, I noticed that nothing had changed. Death occurred regularly right in front of me, just as it had prior to my move. Seeing someone get shot, stabbed, or subjected to other horrible occurrences was an everyday event. In the projects/ghetto where I lived, a person had no way out—there was no escaping that cycle where the same negative driving forces pushed the next generations. It was a time warp that all who lived there endured. The only way I could escape was through education or college. When I entered ninth grade, I had an English teacher named (if I remember correctly) Mrs. Wilson. She was a beautiful lady and one of the most caring teachers that I know. One day, Mrs. Wilson approached me and changed my focus on how I saw life. She asked me if I would be attending the local high school, which was about three miles away from where I lived, called Howard High School. I answered yes. She told me that I had the ability to attend the top high school in Chattanooga and certainly one of the top high schools in the state of Tennessee—Kirkman Vocational Technology High—located seven miles across town. She asked me to test for entry and said I should think about attending this school. Up to that point, *no one* had ever told me I had the ability to do anything. I tested and was accepted into that school.

Over the next three years, I had to travel to my high school by any way possible—walk or thumb a ride. I did extremely well in school, and I graduated. After graduating from high school, though, I found myself still trapped in the projects/ghetto with no way out. There was one road that led to employment for an uneducated person or someone possessing a high school diploma, and I headed down that road. I was very familiar with this road, and I knew where it was going to end because so many traveled that road before me. One thing I had was a great understanding of the word *vision* because I learned this during my stay in Graham, Alabama, from my aunt, uncle, and grandmother; I desired to be somebody. Therefore, many of us possessed tunnel vision, including me, because there was no positive outlook that I could see, so my eyes would focus straight ahead, afraid to turn to the left, afraid to turn to the right, afraid I would bump into the side of the tunnel, fearful of bumping into the blinders and shields that protected each side.

Therefore, I thought the only road was looking straight ahead and following the footsteps that had come before me. One day, as I was walking that same path, I had a paradigm shift. According to my internet search, a paradigm shift is *a dramatic new way of thinking or seeing something*. A paradigm is a shift that happens when the standard method of thinking or doing something is replaced by something new and is adapted by several people. Paradigm shifts have happened in our modern world and will continue to happen.

One day I was walking down that road, and I accidentally removed my tunnel vision blinders and shifted my paradigms. As I continued walking down that road, I thought of a poem written by Robert Frost called *The Road Not Taken*. Typically, my focus was solely on that narrow road and path, and I would walk with my eyes closed, careful not to bump the side of the tunnel, and I was good at that, since I traveled that path often.

But as I walked down that path that day, I closed my eyes and daydreamed for a few seconds. I was completely shocked when I turned my head to the center, opened my eyes, and noticed the road in front of me looked different. I saw roads going to the left with very few footsteps and roads going to the right with more footsteps than the left. At that time, being frozen in the middle of the fork in the road, I had to make a decision. This immediately presented risks and uncertainty. The path straight ahead was all that I knew, and I did not know that I had other options. The thought of risks scares each one of us because of the uncertainty. We are afraid of change because we are taught this is how it should be. I was presented with two notions—continue straight or take a risk and go left or right.

I was afraid to do anything but follow the road straight ahead. But I only had one chance to make the right choice. What should I do? It was clear that risks were involved, but I turned left. Then I saw other roads veer off this one and paused for a second as an imaginary bus came by to pick me up, and the sign read *Navy*. I started to realize that I had more than one option. For every option available, there are several opportunities created; however, we all must make the right choice on whatever path we choose. In Robert Frost's poem, most chose to take the road most traveled. I decided not to.

This all started from the feeling I had of being loved in Graham, Alabama. It continued with my ninth-grade English teacher telling me that I had the ability to do something with my life. And, most importantly, it became real through my willingness to take risks and roads that others were not taking.

Regardless of where a person came from, how bad their situation or circumstances, or the societal odds against them and previous generations—if we learn to love and push our past perceptions aside, we can make a difference in the lives of many youths and young adults. We must let them know that options and opportunities are awaiting them. We must help them make the right choice. Sometimes this may lead to a person making several bad decisions, but I believe we all make bad decisions, and we all fail, but the most important thing is to get back up, continue to try, and focus on making the right decision. This is why I created the JC Cooley Options and Opportunities/The Choice Program. It has been said that it takes a village to raise one child, and our community of "villagers" should lift people up and help show them and most importantly guide them to the right path.

CHAPTER TWO

CHALLENGES

WE CAN ALL AGREE that there will be obstacles and challenges in the face of adversity and when things are not going as planned. Even though we think our plan is our plan, we must quickly learn that everything we do requires approval for success from our Lord and Savior.

Are you willing to sacrifice your beliefs, or do you stand by your convictions? I believe that teamwork and confidence in ourselves is required. Therefore, one mindset should be focused on the love of others, and this requires us to work together, have a vision, develop an understanding, and focus on teamwork as the goal.

I believe in birthrights. Birthrights are confidence, courage, hope, belief, and most importantly, faith. What's in the heart of this Black man is to honestly provide for my family and display a moral compass, always trying to do the right thing in everything I do.

In my opinion, we all have a higher power with God and must be a great leader. One of the names in the Bible that comes to mind is Job. Job lost faith even though the Lord blessed him with family, wealth, understanding, and (I believe) focus. But sometimes when we receive these blessings, we forget we are the orchestra of the decisions we make, and we take them for granted. God has to humble us and remove some blessings he brought into our life because we misunderstood our purpose. Job learned the hard way; he lost everything. Everything was taken away in the blink of an eye because he lost faith. Job lost focus.

I lost focus earlier in my life, and my greatest joy is that these blessings came from God, and He took them away. The lessons I learned are based on upbringing, trials, and tribulations that we experience in life; these often lead us to our core values. Our core values and ethics are what we believe is right or wrong. I can now honestly state that, in my heart, there is confidence, courage, hope, belief, and most importantly faith.

What's in the heart of this Black man is understanding that our true values are built on a foundation that was laid before us, which include the lessons from our ancestors and surroundings; we have an opportunity to redefine our destinies.

In conclusion, what's in the heart of this Black man is love of God, family, people, and even strangers.

CHAPTER THREE

START AND FINISH DATE (SEASONS)

I BELIEVE, IN THE heart of a Black man, he must be willing to change. In the heart of this Black man, I had to realize that situations change like the seasons. Therefore, we must be willing to accept change and understand that there is a start and finish date with everything in life.

In life, the seasons consist of summer, fall, winter, and spring, and it is the job of the seasons to change. God sometimes plants seasonable people in our hearts and lives, people who remain for only a short time. Many times, we get attached to that person, not thinking that we might need to transition into another season; it is God's purpose and plan, after all. This can be disappointing because we come across people and situations that we think are part of a lifetime destination. However, I believe God sends people and situations to teach, guide, and focus us, to center us on His plan.

Before I get too far into this chapter, I want to explain my definitions of "destination" and "destiny," which I believe have distinctly different meanings.

Every step we are given, every path we take, and every journey we seek has a start and finish date. Every destination we are on, including our very own lives, has a start and finish date. And life is a series of destinations that keep us on our path to one day reach our destiny.

When we enter high school, for example, our goal is to finish in four years or less. I call this our early destination. (Remember, I said destination, not destiny.) We must complete this destination to be prepared for our next destination, be it college, military service, or entering the workforce, to gain life lessons and building blocks needed to reach our destiny.

I believe these building blocks are vision, understanding, and focus. As we grow and mature, we sharpen our vision to discern what we want to become. We reduce some of the mistakes we made earlier in life because we gained knowledge from our decisions, both the good and bad. Therefore, our understanding increases. But for us to continue to grow, we must remain focused.

And to accomplish our goals and reach our destiny in whatever timelines we have been given, we also must have short-term, mid-term, and long-term plans.

During a high school presentation, I had pointed messages for the graduating senior class.

I said, "Seniors, your high school destination will end soon. But if you have not planned on your next destination or journey, you may have some problems. Because after graduation, life may be different."

I continued, "Right now, I believe probably many of you are on a destination that you have become accustomed to. Your four years of high school are now in the past. Once you walk across the stage, that destination is over." As I mentioned earlier, focus is key, as it relates to being prepared for your next destination. You have to be strong enough and focused enough to figure out when it is time to get off that proverbial train and know when the ride is coming to an end. You do not want to get too comfortable and miss your stop. You do not want to catch yourself saying, "I know I finished high school or college, but if I fail this class, I can stay another semester."

Bottom line is, you better be prepared for potential future endeavors. There will be several destinations for which you must prepare. So how do we reach our destiny? Through a lifetime of learning, gaining knowledge, and creating a foundation as big as we can get it and through focus, which is key to our successes and to fulfilling our dreams.

Remember, a series of destinations leads us to our destiny. Where will your paths lead you? Most importantly, there is a thing called "destination disease," where you want to stay on your current path even though you know that journey has ended. If you stay only because it's comfortable, it becomes a disease and inhibits growth.

We must find the uniqueness within every one of us to stay on track and reach our destiny. Not our *destination*, our *destiny*. Sometimes, we walk down a path and get sidetracked and thrown off course. We get too comfortable and decide this is where we need to be. But return to your foundation, which I hope you will build as big as possible. Go back your uniqueness because God has already determined your purpose but you must understand your unique purpose for God's goal for you.

I believe the Lord has remade me, and he will remake you if you allow him to. He has given me focus on my destination, and along the way, He brought me to deliver this message to each and every last one of you.

Each of us has our own purpose, a path we must reach, the end of a destiny we must fulfill. Follow and complete your own destiny. That may take a lifetime.

As for me, with this new understanding, I know I have not finished my path, but I do understand that life is full of circles, cycles, phases, and stages; these are the lessons we learn to understand God's purpose for our lives.

I know I am still on my path. I have not reached my finish date. It ain't over yet.

We will face trials, tribulations, uncertainties, and doubt. To be successful, we must be willing to endure the changes that come our way and be focused on adjusting to change as it comes. What's in the heart of this Black man is perseverance, willingness to understand, and willing to give my life to our Savior and understand that service before self is the most important thing in a man's life.

CHAPTER FOUR

LOVE

LOVE EVERYTHING AND EVERYBODY.

Every person wants to be loved, regardless of what is going on in their lives. We all desire a partner who understands our particular needs and wants. We all have individual goals and a perceived purpose based on life experiences and our understanding of the "now." Our mindset and what we believe are the most valuable things to us "now" are most important.

We often fail to understand that change will occur, but we must be cognizant of the things that happened yesterday but not live the past. Our focus needs to be current for today, but we always have to be prepared for tomorrow which is change. No one can determine the events that are going to happen in the next day; the data we have is a prediction based on the current moment. Therefore, I believe flexibility and change should be expected because we know what is going on today—or the "now"—and we might not understand the possibilities for tomorrow.

I believe every Black man desires a partner or mate that he can learn from, acknowledge, and grow with . He should be looking for someone with extremely high standards, someone strong enough to voice their opinions about what is right and wrong. He must believe they have his back and that they trust and support him. I believe he must be willing to share a relationship fifty-fifty but still maintain the overall decision-making as long as it is in the best interest of the family. He also must provide a sense of security for his family regardless of the situations and circumstances they will encounter.

I believe a Black man must feel comfortable with his potential soulmate. For his potential soulmate to truly understand his desires, they must be capable of understanding his needs. I believe these needs are not particularly sexual, even though in most Black men's hearts and minds, that may be the most important aspect while choosing his mate. I believe they must have a connection to evolve.

My definition of "evolve" is similar to the theory of evolution. As we grow and learn, we have to adapt and accept things that we would not have usually accepted because we did not have the understanding before we evolved. Learning to evolve is so important in a relationship, and this is a hinderance in many of my fellow Black men, just like it was with me.

God's plan is for us to grow together, learn together, and accept together. I believe these are the true facets to determine what it's in the heart of a man, not just a Black man but every man. The theory of evolution is real, and every Black man needs to carefully choose his true soulmate in life. We must withstand the negative things that are going to happen and not quit when things are at their lowest point; change is inevitable. When there is a life-changing situation, we may decide the person we chose as our soulmate is not the person we thought they were. I believe a Black man should truly understand the person and character they choose from the beginning. We all will change mentally, physically, and spiritually, but I believe we all must be willing to accept the change.

I believe evolving is growing together, strategizing together, planning together, sharing true feelings together, and respecting each other. Respect—regardless of where someone's from, what they believe, or what they think—is fundamental in a relationship. Respect is necessary for character evolution.

Evolving means opening up to your mate, being able to laugh and cry together. Most importantly, evolving means having a plan for today, tomorrow, next week, and for generations to come. With love and understanding, we must provide an example for the future.

Starting in 1619, slavery forced Black men from their native country, placed them on ships, and located them in a foreign land with no rights for generations and generations. In some places in America, I believe many people still consider us slaves and have not fully accepted Abraham Lincoln's Emancipation Proclamation, signed January 1, 1865. But we have learned so much from our past. We must continue to strive to be free men and believe that our voices will one day be considered equal by the rest of society. With over 400 years of being enslaved, we as Black men have not and will not forget where we came from.

We will continue to teach our future generations that we have been battling the triumph of white supremacy and colonization that has tried and will continue to try to suppress our memories of what our forefathers experienced. We must also teach them not to dwell on the past of our forefathers but to always look ahead at how we can continue to move forward and be leaders in a world where everyone is free and of equal value, regardless of race, creed, color, sexuality, or religion.

What's in the heart of this Black man is something we don't talk about enough—OSD, which stands for "oppression, suppression, and depression." We as Black men had to endure masters who controlled our every movement, thought, and being. We built many nations with our backs, arms, and sweat, and we endured weakness. We had to sit back every step of the way and watch our women be raped and taken advantage of, and there was nothing we could do because we had no power, and our hearts were destroyed because we were helpless and considered less than a man. We were not allowed to get an education. We were merely considered a mule or donkey, which is an ass.

As we evolved from slavery in 1865 under Abraham Lincoln, most states, especially Texas, did not allow us to get any news or information that African Americans were legally free men. The name Freeman comes from Abraham Lincoln and the Emancipation Proclamation. In other states, we did not get the opportunity to celebrate being a free man, which did not even honor the negro as free men until more than two years later. We call that Juneteenth.

I do not believe we are free men. I do not believe the American society truly recognizes us as full men. We must fight not in physical war but through vision, understanding, and focus, and by shifting the focus from White America to America, because Black people built this country and the foundation of what America stands for. We are truly Americans as well, and our contributions generationally, today, and tomorrow make us a fundamental part of the backbone of America.

I believe what's in the heart of a Black man should be the focus of not just Black Americans but all Americans who wish to ensure that what's in our hearts should be in the hearts of every American, regardless of skin color. We must get rid of our focus on the past and understand the future and focus on what we all as Americans can create for tomorrow.

What's in the heart of this Black man is love, compassion, reason, and the vision to love one another regardless of race, religion, creed, or color.

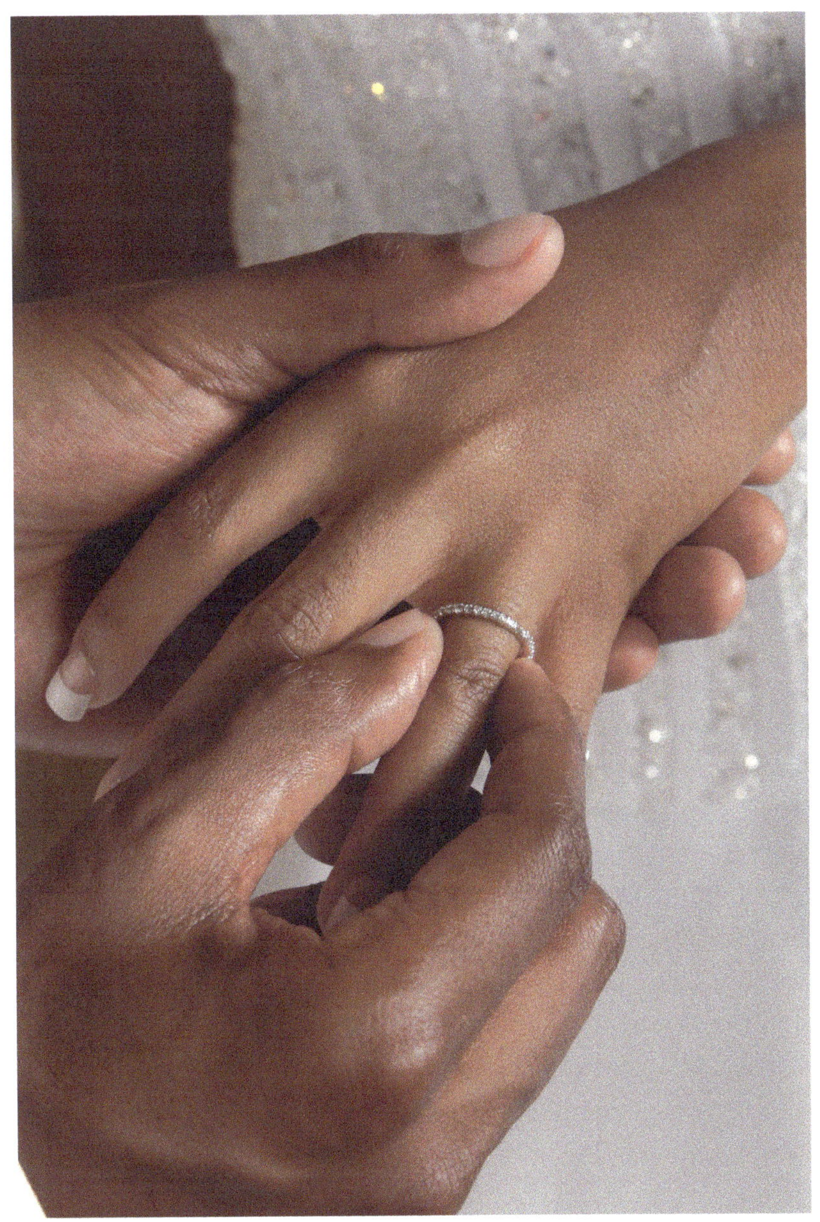

CHAPTER FIVE

ULTIMATE LOVE

LOVE AND COMPASSION ARE the creeds that every man should have, regardless of their color.

As we truly understand ourselves, we realize that we all have a selfish nature. What I mean is, we base our decision-making on what we learned in the past, and we believe that is the way of life because that is the only way we know. Sometimes, we get a wake-up call about who we are and what we are here to do, and we believe that life will never deliver our true soulmate; perhaps this mindset stemmed from our upbringing. Therefore, we believe that the purpose of love does not exist and will never be achieved.

We wander through life with a hardened heart, never looking for true love because it does not exist in our minds. Our Lord and Savior already knows our thoughts, desires, wants, and needs, and out of the blue, he sends a unique person into our lives. As is true in my experience, the man receiving God's gifts may be completely stunned or caught off guard; his mindset and focus may not be on meeting somebody who can soften his heart.

Marriage exists between a man and a woman. But I have learned to understand that love has no color, no sex, and no mathematic combination; whether two men or two women, it is love. I have become nonjudgmental when it comes to love, not saying that my beliefs have changed.

When we find that mate—in my case, my wife—we have to be one-hundred-percent committed to how we fell in love with that person. We've all had misconceptions about love before, but our heart understands when our body, soul, and mind quivers at our ultimate love. This feeling displays an unquestionable commitment to that person, and when we fully commit, we never want to do anything to hurt that person. As we grow with our chosen mate, we experience trials and tribulations and many challenges that can cause us to veer on different paths. The terrain can get rocky, the roads widen, and there is no bridge to join the couple; if this happens, it may be easy to forget the connection, passion, and love we stemmed from. Never burn or destroy the bridge. It will be almost impossible to reconnect or get back on the same road, and those dreams from the ultimate love story can be hard to find once they're lost.

Our focus may change over time, and if we are not able to bridge the gap, we grow further and further apart. If we are not growing together, we're growing apart.

We must always remind each other how important it felt from the first day we fell in love, how important that love still is, and how important it is to stay on the path to our collective dreams. Love is like a chicken and an egg. What came first, the chicken or the egg? As we become more seasoned, we grow together, of equal mind, body, and soul. We must develop the philosophy of being *yoked*. Here's what I mean: If we drop an egg, it's going to splatter. If we establish ultimate love and are allowing the egg to harden and boil, then the egg becomes a yoke. We should always remember that when we commit to our ultimate love and partner, we want to make sure that the egg is hard-boiled, and we are locked into the ultimate love we had for life.

What's in the heart of this Black man is commitment.

If we truly love someone, from the beginning of the relationship, we have to look at it as the flame from the 1800s—if we don't keep it burning, the flame will die. We must keep the flame burning; this requires continuous kerosene as the fuel to the fire. Ultimate love requires we focus on what lit the flames in the first place.

Once the light goes out, many of us find ourselves in the darkness, trying to find another light, but there is no replacement light for the original light. That requires communication between both individuals. In my case, I want to communicate with my wife when I experience challenges, and she can help us compromise on the best solution to stay true to our ultimate love. For us to be totally at ease with a decision, we want to blame our mate for why we might have made the decision that we made. I call this the "victim mentality." This goes both ways in a relationship. If we truly lock into someone else's vision or decision, we do not always make the best decision realistically that coincides with our true feelings. We want to blame someone else for things that don't go our way.

In a relationship, we have to accept responsibility for our role and not proclaim to be a victim of the outcome. In ultimate love, we must always maintain our individuality and make choices or decisions that are in the best interest of our beliefs and faith, not based on another person's heart.

Sometimes we may not come to a conclusion, and we still lean toward acting on the desires of our heart. Desire is a want; it is not a need. There is a total difference between wants and needs. As Abraham Maslow stated in the hierarchy of needs, there are requirements needed to survive. There are physiological needs, safety needs, love and belonging needs, esteem needs, and self-actualization needs in men, and it is no different for Black men. These needs are so important to him and his family or mate that he would do anything in his power to protect them. However, the negative side of this is that sometimes he may lose focus and turn to his desires—to his wants.

A man or woman who lacks understanding about the differences between needs and wants may let their desires win. This destroys relationships, especially in the Black community.

Having ultimate love requires a mate who is truly one-hundred-percent invested in the commitment. We have to prevent the relationship from being compromised so that we don't lose our ultimate love. But even if we can rekindle all that we have built in the relationship, it will never be the same; once we lose the bond, it is almost impossible to regain it all back. We get older, become more seasoned, grow wiser, and truly understand that love is not all physical, not all emotional, and not all spiritual—it is a combination of all three—and that is what being yoked is all about.

What's in the heart of this Black man is maintaining my ultimate love with my soulmate, withstanding the trials and tribulations we face, and focusing on our needs over our wants, ensuring that we maintain the foundations of God, family, and service as it relates to my Lord and Savior.

CHAPTER SIX

GOD'S GREATEST GIFT TO THIS BLACK MAN

AS I SIT BACK and think about my six decades of living, I now understand that my philosophy and beliefs before were not truly God's plan for me. After two failed marriages, many trials and tribulations, and two near-death experiences, I understand that God has a way to capture our attention and focus. My original plan was designed for a single man who looked at life from a single man's vantage point. God always reminds us of his purpose for us, and if we don't follow it, I believe He sometimes makes sure that we are not around or do not have the shield of armor that He provided us and blessed us with carrying.

I believe God's greatest gift to a man is a woman. It is my belief that, in the hearts of many Black men, we are greedy, and we believe we need many of everything—that includes soulmates. This reminds me of "The Songs of Solomon." Even though man might have everything he wants, God was showing him that true love cannot be bought with riches.

Solomon had over five hundred wives, but he did not have his true soulmate. I believe God planned not just for a Black man but for every man to have the right soulmate to do God's work. Many Black men, including myself, lacked understanding and were not able to receive God's full blessing. We did not have the right soulmate in our lives to fulfill His plan. Many of us still do not (and may never) because we cannot get rid of the idea of having many. I believe every man (especially a Black man) wants to figure things out and do them on his own terms, but that may not have been God's intention for him.

We all make mistakes in our relationships and take our perceived soulmate for granted. Based on my understanding, I do not believe a relationship or marriage can be successful without the right soulmate. God chooses you to lead and direct the purpose for others; He wants that individual to lead by example based on His purpose for choosing you. I believe a Black man wants a soulmate who has his back and truly loves him for everything he stands for and believes in.

I do not believe true love exists unless our chosen soulmate believes in our purpose, philosophy, and vision as it relates to God. It's similar to the story of David; his father Jesse had eight sons, and God already proclaimed that the next King of Israel would come from Jesse's family, and he sent Samuel to anoint that king. Jesse sent seven of his sons, who were big and strong, and Samuel tried to anoint each one of the sons; however, he did not get God's blessing for one of these seven sons. Samuel said to Jesse, "The Lord has not chosen these." So, he asked, "Are these all the sons you have?" "There is still the youngest," Jesse answered, "but he is tending." Samuel said, "Send for him; we will not sit down until he arrives." Samuel poured the oil on his head, and God told Samuel that this was the next king of Israel.

My point is, I believe in the heart of a Black man, we choose early and make many mistakes. We see aspects of a person we believe to be good for us without really understanding the surroundings and potential that God has placed on us. As far as being a man, husband, or provider, we are greedy, but this is not the plan that God has for us. In my case, after two failed marriages (and four wonderful kids), I realize I was never in love with the wives I chose because they were not sent by God. However, I did love them. God allowed me to make these mistakes, empty-hearted but successful as a Black man. Anybody who looked at me, seeing what I had accomplished, would think that I was successful, but in my heart and mind, I was unhappy because I did not have God's blessings.

I believe this is a major problem in the African American community.

Men will figure out that no man is an island, and you must have support. In the heart of this Black man, after going through several struggles, including near-death experiences, I thought that God had no purpose for me on this Earth. But God reminded me that I had true purpose. He led the way to my path and to my soulmate.

While I can't comment on others' experiences, I can share mine. Change was required for me to understand that I had purpose and needed to fulfill God's purpose. I completely refocused and gave my life, mind, body, and soul to the Lord. I was going to do it His way, but I was not exactly sure what His plan was. Shortly later, I met this young lady at the mall. We innocently chatted, but after a while, I understood this was the first change I needed to make to meet the purpose the Lord had for me. As I understood this person more, I was like the Holy Ghost. I never felt that way before, and all I wanted to do was be with this woman. I was so grateful to God for this opportunity. I realized He created her for me to fulfill his promise to me. She became my soulmate, and after seventeen years, she still is today. I had to understand and grow into this great gift that God had provided me.

I had to grow into everything he visually showed me. He knew I was stubborn. I had to figure out that a man who finds his soulmate or wife finds a good thing! We have to trust our soulmate wholeheartedly and believe in them. And they truly have to believe in us, but most importantly, both of our beliefs in our higher power must be the same.

In the heart of many Black men, there are still issues of trust. I had to believe in God and in the soulmate that He chose for me. I am happy, I have found new life in the purpose that I am living,

I have found my true soulmate, I am one-hundred-percent yoked, and I have dedicated the rest of my life to making sure that we do all we can to bring joy and happiness to everyone we meet.

Trust has to be earned completely, and you have to know that every time a portion of trust is violated, it reverts back to the original setting, and that is still the standard in our society. Most of us do not even trust God. God placed in my heart that I needed to trust Him, and the only way to succeed was to trust the soulmate He chose for me. I had to open up my heart and allow myself visually and mentally to grow. It was a challenge because I was scared and afraid. Once I committed to what God said, every time I was with her, I looked at my soulmate, and I was falling in love with her. Every time I thought about her, I was thinking of God. He created her just for me.

We, as Black men, must be able to commit to another and have faith in the Lord and whoever the Lord has chosen for us. As we grow and become closer to the Lord, we become closer to the purpose and become "yoked." It is not about me; it's about having the best mind, body, and soul.

That is what is in the heart of this Black man, and I believe that it should be in the heart of every man and every Black man—submission to God's plan requires us to change our focus and accept love for everything and everybody. I did not feel worthy, but I believe I am worthy now. This complete refocus of my life has made me the person that I am today—over seventeen years.

I know my selfish ways, conceited ways, and lack of trust in the past was not the key to success today. I promised myself that once I accepted God's new plan for me, I would follow that plan and do all that he empowered me to do in partnership with my soulmate. Our commitment is to be better and make everyone we come in contact with better as well. So, God's greatest gift to this Black man was to have an open heart, to believe in myself, to accept others as they are, and to not live a greedy life. I now strive to be the person He created me to be.

My heart believes we should not look at things as they are true today but live life how it should be tomorrow for our happiness and our future generations. You have to have vision, understanding, and focus.

CHAPTER SEVEN

INSECURITIES

IT'S SO IMPORTANT, I'LL say it again: we should not live life too focused on today; we should focus on what we envision for tomorrow. This is very hard as it relates to what is in the heart of Black men because we have endured so many things over the last 400 years that it has created an insecurity mindset. Black men have never been considered full men; even today, we are not considered equal because of our origin and race, and it's perceived that we aren't intelligent like our White counterparts. Even after generations of hard work, solid work ethics, and education in the Western world, this is still not enough; there is a stigma and stereotypical ideas that Black men are lazy and will always expect a handout.

Therefore, I believe that we must do everything in our power to ensure that we have vision, understanding, and focus. One day, our grandkids and our great-great grandkids and future generations will understand that they are equal to everyone else on this Earth, regardless of their color, creed, or religion. For me, these thoughts stem from thinking that no one cared for or loved me as a child—not even my family—because the word *love* was never said in my household. It was assumed that they did. But I grew up without positive inspiration or an understanding that I might one day be of importance and welcomed to be who I am.

I was young and naïve, and many of us still are. I remember watching a Jack Nicholson film that made me believe that everyone has their own value, and no one person is better than the rest. We all have our strengths and weaknesses.

As a Black man, we have always been shown that we lack worthiness, and we are not important. Many of us are afraid to look at into others' eyes. Most of us look down when we are talking and don't make eye contact because we are still made to feel inferior and do not want to cause any problems that will affect our family or ourselves. In today's America, most of the focus is based on our inferior complex, and most of the laws were created to control the Black and Brown population growth. Laws are created to control the twenty-first-century thought process, and men and women can love anyone regardless of race, creed, or sexual orientation. Older generations are focused on returning to the original Western civilizations, where none of these thoughts existed because of fear. I do not understand why anyone would want to go backward and not forward; people are scared of change, but it is inevitable.

Change is going to happen regardless. *Behavior* plus *vision* equals *change*. I also believe that *behavior* plus *intolerable pain* leads to *change*. This happens to older generations focused on the past and forward-thinkers. We can mature with our visions—growing with the change—or we can learn with intolerable pain. Regardless, we can change with the *brain* or change with *pain*. Change is going to happen. As for Black men, we had to endure both change with the brain and change with pain.

Sometimes we choose less than what we were capable of because of our insecurities, not wanting to cause or create problems because of our external perceptions as people of color. We accept *less than* because we do not want to fight the challenges of racism, stereotypes, and societal stigma. We as Black men sometimes quit and hope to turn it over to the next generation to solve that problem.

For me, making sure I chose the right soulmate, who understood my insecurities and her value, helped ease the pain and create a new vision for me and our future generations. We practice identifying both of our insecurities and then decide. In the heart of this Black man is an understanding of what we are willing to sacrifice and an agreement to stand by our convictions. To truly make a difference, we must be willing to die for what we believe in. Standing by our beliefs removes the power from what others say about us. We must acknowledge our insecurities to make them go away.

To remove insecurities, it requires that me and my soulmate agree to being a team; it's more powerful than being individuals. Teamwork requires respect and consideration of both peoples' wishes. Therefore, we should not rely on other people's approval to feel or think. This does not solve the problem of insecurity. It comes from what we think about ourselves and what we believe in our heart, mind, body, and soul. If we lock in on what other people think about us, self-confidence does not increase because we're constantly seeking approval from others. We must not need approval from anyone beyond God and our soulmate (and ourselves). If we seek advice outside of that, we are going to have problems.

Our feelings originate from a lack of confidence and a need for approval, which results in insecurities. But we must stay true to our values. It is important to reflect on our past, but we cannot live inside it. We must understand who we were yesterday and what we endured while we were there. Paying close attention to who we are today and keeping an open mind allows for setting tomorrow's visions, making us better individually and as a team. We must do this to lead future generations, set our legacy, and decrease insecurity.

The next generation must understand, from our guidance, that change is inevitable. We must show them that a current situation does not determine our final destination—unless we choose that ending. We have a destiny to fulfill, and insecurities must not be the downfall of our legacy.

Where there is no vision, we will perish because we have no way to understand our purpose, and our main goal is what we need to focus on. We must always be able to see past the tip of our noses. We must be able to focus on our abilities to excel and overcome our fears and insecurities. We must be able to forgive the past. We must be able to understand that the many prejudices that occurred during previous generations (and many that are still occurring during our lifetime today) were temporary setbacks, but I believe we must teach our future generations that they are the change—the future. We must learn to love, not hate.

Our insecurities must not dominate our vision, understanding, and focus. Continue to believe that change will come; one day, the world's people will be considered equal.

CHAPTER EIGHT

REFLECTIONS

ATTITUDE

OUR SINGLE GREATEST GIFT is the freedom to choose our attitude. Your attitude is more important than knowledge, education, background, wealth, position, talent, or appearance. It is even more powerful than what other people think, say, or do. It will make or break a team, a company, a person, a relationship, and a home.

"I am convinced that life is 5 percent what happens to me and 95 percent how I choose to look and react to it. And so, it is with you. . . . Your attitude is your choice!"

—ELLEN A. MILLER

"Love is patient, Love is kind, and is not jealous; love does not brag and is not arrogant, does not act unbecomingly; it does not seek its own, is not provoked, does not take into account a wrong suffered, does not rejoice in unrighteousness, but rejoices with the truth; bears all things, believes all things, hopes all things, endures all things love never fails."

—1 CORINTHIANS 13:4-8

"To enjoy good health, to bring true happiness to one's family, to bring peace to all, one must first discipline and control one's own mind. If a man can control his mind he can find the way to Enlightenment, and all wisdom and virtue will naturally come to him."

—BUDDHA

Every person must make their own choices and take their own paths. We are born with all the tools to do so at birth. We call these birthrights—confidence, courage, hope, belief, and most importantly, faith. I believe this leads to our destiny in life. We must consult with our Lord and Savior on all decisions as it relates to our destiny. Our Lord and Savior will provide guidance and direction. Then we can continue our path, knowing that our decisions are based on our Lord and Savior's direction. I believe we should be thrilled, pleased, grateful, and most importantly, honored with our choices and God's guidance.

I believe we are born with a choice. We either enter this world crying instantly, or we enter this world silence, in need of help immediately (no cry equals a spank on the rear end). That is how we enter this world; therefore, the choice is up to every individual and unique soul.

Options lead to opportunities (potential successes), and opportunities lead us to making the right choice. This choice helps us to create the road map in pursuing our destiny.

This chapter is a compilation of sayings and proverbs and is designed to be used as a reference, to carry in your pocket, referred to often, taken out, read, and remembered. Through repetitive reading and reflection, the information will be engrained in your mind. Work with this chapter one statement at a time.

The pathway to all successes is through your "I am." Dream and plan for your future through actions. Call it to your conscious mind by saying "I am" going to do this—not "I might," or even "I will try." These are negative connotations, which may lead to failure. We must program our brain with the positive thoughts of "I am," "I will," and "I know I am going to do this." Your life will come together when you decide it should. The decision is yours and yours alone. No one else can do this for you.

I believe our brain is the most powerful computer in the world, and nothing compares with its ability. The question is, how are we programing our brains? This will determine our ability to perform tomorrow's tasks and to live a happy life. But unlike a computer, in which we download a program once, we must download our thoughts often, until our conscious mind has memorized the information.

Humans have trouble with change because it is all about attitude. Embrace change as a learning curve, a teacher, and the key to success. If we are not happy with today, then we must change the way we think and act. Time is our most precious asset. It is the only possession we own; do not waste it. How we plan to use this time will determine our future. We must develop a plan of actions, write it down, commit to the plan, and focus on executing the plan. Time will not stop, slow down, or wait on us, so it is in our best interest to use our time wisely.

When we forgive, we relieve our mind of the baggage we are carrying. When we tell someone they hurt us, we relieve their mind by offering honest opinions and forgiving them. This is a path to positive thinking and mental peace. Our emotions, intellect, and will are the keys to positive thinking. We cannot program our mind to dismiss negative thoughts. Those negative thoughts must be replaced with positive thoughts. Practice this because it is not only the secret to obtaining and achieving our goals, but it is the key to a happy life. We should train our mind to stay positive. Start today. Only think positive thoughts and achieve positive actions. A man is but the product of his thoughts;

what he thinks, he becomes. What is in a man's heart will surely come out his mouth. Instead of dwelling on what we do not have, we must think of all the wonderful things we do have. Express appreciation to all, and be grateful for this life.

We can control our emotions, for they are an action of our mind. Note that love is not an emotion but an activity. Actively love everyone and everybody, for this will bring mental peace. Life's temptations sometimes cause emotions to flare out of control. We must always be aware of these temptations and fight off the negative thoughts driving this action. Remember, practice makes perfect. So, what are you practicing?

It will take a great deal of courage to dream your biggest life dream. There will be many roadblocks along life's journey. It will take courage, risk, and understanding to get past these obstacles. If we think "I can't," then we won't, but when we think "I can," it will happen. Continue to dream big, think big, and be big with positive thoughts and attitude and accomplish each goal one at a time. This is the key to enlightenment.

We must surround ourselves with people of the highest character. These people are chosen family. We must dismiss those people of low character but try to help all people by being a great leader who sets an excellent example for others. Each day, we must write down our goal of accomplishments and keep this list going throughout our lives, always adding more items and crossing off as we go. Never put off to tomorrow what can be accomplished today. Let tomorrow's list be full of new challenges. Plan—do not just let it happen. We are capable of accomplishing anything we set our mind to. We must not sell ourselves short.

We were given a mind that can do anything. We have all the brain power we need. It is how we program our mind and how we use it that makes an enlightened person. Practice makes perfect, so what are you practicing? What we conceive and believe will be ours to achieve.

Compassion is to deeply care about everything and everyone. Compassion is an expression of love. The more love and kindness we give others, the more we will receive. An unhealthy lifestyle limits our mind's ability to achieve our goals. Managing our health is our responsibility, and nobody else can do this for us. A healthy body leads to a healthy mind. Knowledge comes from what we learned from our surroundings, education, upbringing, beliefs, successes, and failures. Knowledge gained is useless unless it can be applied and utilized. Understanding is applying that knowledge, and knowledge and understanding provide the *key* to finding wisdom. Have you obtained the necessary knowledge to help you find wisdom? We have all the power we need to build a beautiful character. But like making a cake, if we leave out one key ingredient (especially sugar), then our cake might be ruined. Are you leaving anything out of your character building?

This brings us to leadership. A manager manages the day-to-day operations and the objectives and goals of the establishment. A leader leads by example. They understand the goals, they understand the people, and they understand what motivates others to be the best they can be. A leader is a person who knows the way, goes the way, and most importantly, shows the way. A leader is built on his/her character. The worst lie we can tell is one to ourselves. Be truthful and honest because a true leader is looked up to and noticed. Set the example, and be honest.

If you knew today was the last day of your life, how would you live it? Life is not supposed to be all work; life is supposed to have pleasure. Stick to a schedule for work, play, and rest. Do not let life happen to you. You should be the one to make it happen. Schedule your time accordingly. Get passionate about more than just one thing. Take time for people and activities that are important to you because life is short, and life will pass you by. Even when you are not here, life will still go on. Always have multiple plans and options for yourself. Options lead to opportunities; opportunities lead to choices. The right choice will lead you to enlightenment and success.

In closing, I believe in Martin Luther King Jr's vision that man should not be judged by the color of his skin, education, skillset, and perceived upbringing. Everything can rely on a person's character. This is what we really need to focus on.

The path we take makes us who we are. Giving our best each day and treating others with respect and kindness—regardless of their external identity—means following the pillars of a person's character—honesty, integrity, and ethics. Remember, we do not have to walk on water; it is how we choose to walk on land that matters. We are not entitled to anything except what we obtained through our own efforts. We must not make others work for us, but with pride and hard work, we can obtain what we seek.

Most people spend a lifetime caught between fear and guilt. These emotions can blind us from our pathway in life. Our destiny is our choice. Mental tools like saying "I am" and obtaining the power of positive thinking help us accomplish our goals. Form a plan, commit to the plan, but most importantly, stay focused. Activate your plan now!

When we are talking, we learn nothing. Listen to others speak; hear them out and then talk. Listen to those who are worthy of attention. Words are more powerful than thoughts. Choose words carefully, and listen carefully and cautiously to others.

Parenting is the toughest job in the world. We must instill positive thinking in our children and be an example for them. Are you truly setting a positive example for your children? Are your parenting skills fair, good, or excellent? Any answer other than *excellent* gives you a failing grade. The example we set may determine the successes and failures we experience as parents and the path for our children. We must ensure we have the right mixture of parenting skills, understanding, and self-control. Remember, parenting is the most important thing we will ever do. Be the example—it is our job and obligation.

I believe humans have the ability to create Heaven on Earth. Our soul is an extension of God. Humans must seek love and compassion and clearly understand what is right and what is wrong. Most importantly, we must respect all living things. All nations must unite in this goal. The human race must learn to love and respect one another and minimize the acts of war.

With the world's financial gains, we can feed the world, build homes, educate the majority of the world, advance medical science, advance technology, and study the universe to help mankind understand what is required for Earth's continued survival. Our past is an illusion in our mind; no one else can see it or feel it. Think of happy memories, and train the mind to get rid of baggage. Negative thoughts destroy happiness. Why let the past influence the future? Seek happiness above all else.

Many of us spend a lifetime caught between fear and guilt. These emotions blind us. We do not have to live in fear or feel guilty about our choices if we always do the best we can.

It is not always about what you know but who you know and who cares to know you. Who do you care to know?

When the Dalai Lama was asked what surprised him most about humanity, he answered, "Man sacrifices his health in order to make money. Then he sacrifices money to recuperate his health. And then he is so anxious about the future that he does not enjoy the present; the result being that he does not live in the present or the future; he lives as if he is never going to die, and then dies having never really lived."

A leader must be able to influence. This is done by setting an example and utilizing strengths and weaknesses. Build trust amongst team members. Leadership is recognizing others' qualities, abilities, and characteristics, and then placing team members in the right positions for the entire organization to be successful. An organization, company, community, and family are weak or strong based on the leaders who guide them.

We cannot live in the past (yesterday), we must live in the now (today), but most importantly, we must prepare for tomorrow (future). It is my opinion that the mind retains about 15 percent of what we hear and 60 percent of what we hear somebody else say. Learning becomes a habit through receptiveness. We must develop great habits to retain old things and help the brain store new, fresh, and mental thoughts.

Repetition helps program the mind. Life's cycles and experiences teach us lessons; we can ignore them or embrace them. We should have fun in our lives, express love, and laugh often. Life should not be a task—it should be a joyful journey. Our choices determine everything about our life. Life can be Heaven on Earth, or it can be hell on Earth. We must always be careful with the decisions we make.

A winner never quits, and a quitter never wins. However, sometimes with a winning attitude we must refocus on the things that are required for us to win. Being kind and always smiling makes it easier to compliment others (even when we are not in the most joyful mood). Kindness is free and does not have a cost to it. Respect is also free. Generosity is free. Asking someone how they are doing might bring happiness to their day. Try and see the good in everyone. Share views, but do not be a critic; compliments should always be positive.

CHAPTER NINE

A BLACK MAN'S POINT OF VIEW: MIND, BODY, AND SOUL

The following are stories from eleven contributing authors.

CAPTAIN (RETIRED)
HERMAN "ARCH" ARCHIBALD

What's in the Heart of This Black Man?

THIS IS A PROFOUND question with multiple levels, phases, and stages. As a Black man who is transitioning from middle-aged years to the old-age stage of life, the passion in my heart is to direct people into understanding how to discover their God-given purpose. I believe, aside from developing a personal relationship with our Lord and Savior Jesus Christ, fulfilling one's purpose is the single most important assignment in life.

So, what is purpose? Oxford Dictionary defines purpose as, "the reason for which something is done or created or for which something exists." From a biblical perspective, purpose is the original intent God created and involves hearing God's specific and personal will for one's life. God gives purpose not just for the individual but also for the generation in which the individual is called to serve. The Bible states in Acts 13:36, "Now when David had served God's purpose in his own generation, he fell asleep; he was buried with his ancestors and his body decayed." This scripture paints a vivid picture of the importance of fulfilling the God-given purpose for one's life. If we accomplish a million things in life but failed to accomplish the assignment that God has given us, then we will have failed life's most important examination.

My first encounter with God's purpose for my life occurred when I was nine years old while attending a small church in Aliceville, Alabama, with Mrs. Virbell Archibald, my grandmother. She was a godly and adorable woman who loved God and always talked about the goodness of God to our family. Grandmother often reminded me that God has a calling on my life, and He has a purpose for me to fulfill. As I watched the pastor of this local church feed God's people with knowledge and understanding, God spoke to my heart and revealed His purpose for my life: I was to become a shepherd to His people. I never heard a loud voice from the sky, nor did I see some great miracle. What I felt was an overwhelming sense of peace that filled my mind and awakened my spirit to the presence of God. This was quite confusing to me because my plan was to become a physician and serve the community. I was a good student, had a plan, and there were no Black physicians in my hometown. God's plan and purpose for me was not what I would have chosen nor was it something that I was excited about fulfilling. There were plenty of preachers in my community, and most of them were not financially stable. Over the years, I would discover firsthand that God knows what's best for us because He created and designed us with a purpose in mind.

The decision to fulfill one's purpose is not an easy decision and it's often lonely. Since your life is not your own and you are on a divine assignment from God, He gets to make the rules. Yet God will not violate our free will; we must choose to submit to God's direction for our life. For example, David experienced insecurities, inadequacies, and failure on the largest of stages. He was forgotten by his father, belittled by his brother, and despised by the king whom he admired. Despite these things, David developed the strength and endurance to serve God's purpose and became a beacon of light and a bridge of hope to his generation.

It has been nearly fifty years since God visited my heart with His divine purpose for me. I understand with a fresh perspective what was said in Jeremiah 3:15, "I will give you pastors according to mine heart, who shall feed you with knowledge and understanding." As the senior pastor of Empowerment Church International in Pensacola, Florida, I help people navigate life's uncertainties by teaching them to think strategically about their life. As the ocean consists of ebbs and flows, so does life. In most cases, our successes are not final nor are our failures fatal. The ones who are obedient to the call of God and prioritize discovering their God-given purpose will best weather life's storms. This Black man's heart is focused on pointing people to God, the creator of everything, and teaching them how to trust Him in the manifestation of their purpose for being born.

JORDAN COLBERT

Pain, Ambition, and Compassion:
The Heart of This Black Man

I AM THE BEATING heart of a man who is both Black and White. According to the one-drop rule, I am the beating heart of a Black man. According to some, which is too many if you care about the opinion of a heart, I beat differently than they do. Speaking from the heart, I can assure you, I do not. As a warrior that beats their chest in victory, I experience a slew of pains, explosions of ambitious ventures, and the compassion to know we all need support to go on.

THE PAINS

My first beat was a miracle of medical misinformation around sterility, which kept me beating to birth. Knowing that is okay, because the beats outside of the womb quickly led to the pains of life for hearts like me. Hearts born to a chaotic world of abandonment, poverty, and abuse tend to struggle to beat for very long. Statistics say they typically stop before twenty-five. Hearts that conflictingly are told, "You are not a White heart," and, "You are not a Black heart," in separate circles, beat to the tune of *Melancholy Blues*.[1] We continue to beat, despite the inevitable suicidal ideations, relationship difficulties, and self-hatred. We weather the typical labels of "nigger" and profiling by police. We navigate these pains, and we beat on. That is, as long as the constricting oppression doesn't block our veins.

---

1   Louis Armstrong & His Hot Seven. (1927). *Melancholy Blues/Keynote Blues* [Album]. OKeh 8496; Parlophone (Australia) A 6391; Parlophone (UK) R 2162; Vocalion 3137

AMBITION IN MY VEINS

I've heard, as much as a heart can, the "only hope I had was selling dope"[2] from my brothers. Hearts in single- and jailed-parent households, particularly in areas of crime juxtaposed to wealth, feel the strong need to prove their worth and strive to thrive despite a lack of expectations. Although poverty and being a minority may require this belief from time to time, my contemporary classmates' hearts guided this heart to other visions through access. Ravenously, I beat with a fervor to surpass those who showed me the fire that burns within Plato's cave. From there on, I beat like a drum solo consistently for twenty hours a day, with only few hours of slow, controlled bongo beats, to match the Virgil-like lifestyle. That ambitious drumbeat led to this heart no longer needing to struggle to sync with their beats. From what I hear of our new role model's mantra, this is known as "started from the bottom, now we're here."[33]

Let me be clear, the strength of my striving heartbeats can also be modeled after my peer within the revered Barack Obama, who rose to prominence during my late adolescence. Knowing that Obama's heart was so full of love and hope for his fellow human gave me the courage to dream as big as a young heart could imagine. When the President of the United States looks like you, a heart can see itself doing great things, especially when that President's journey has been well-documented, and it resembles your own. That type of representation sharpened the determination to succeed and was instilled by my classmates' beating hearts.

---

2   Wale. (2011). *Ambition* [Album]. Maybach Music Group; Allido Records; Warner Bros. Records.

3   Drake. (2013). Started from the Bottom. On Nothing Was the Same [Album]. Aspire; Young Money; Cash Money; Republic.

COMPASSION

We hearts that hold pain and convert that to ambition understand the need to heal. From my humble cardiac opinion, the ability to beat compassionately is the most important component of this heart. The factors leading to the successful and healthy heart pontificating here today inculcated the integral nature of supporting those who need it. According to Malcom X, it's an obligation for us to build our brothers up, and that will only be achieved through compassionate support. It's obligatory to engage in heart-to-heart connections that remind us we're not alone in the struggle, we all face barriers moving forward, and we must help each other move toward a better future. All of this is what's inside of me—the heart of this Black man.

DR. LESTER FREEMAN, MD

WHAT'S IN THE HEART OF THIS BLACK MAN?

MY PARENTS WERE ALWAYS the guiding force in making me the person and the man I am today. Any errors that I've made and will make or internal flaws that I was born with are mine and mine alone . . . and it's because I strayed from the path I was on by my loving and supportive family.

Anything complimentary or congratulatory that's been said to me or about me is due to the values and important life lessons that were carefully planted and cultivated by my parents; a few of those qualities that I've been blessed with are industrious listener, vigilance, and determination. One cannot be successful or competent with any of these gifts and skills.

I read a very inspirational poem on the wall at—of all places—my closest friend's barbershop a couple of decades ago. It talked about determination and how that singularly is the most powerful, reliable, and quantifiable predictor of success.

In that poem, they talked about how some individuals may have more talent, be blessed with more gifts, or may have been born into an affluent family that has the financial resources that most people lack; however, when all those advantages mentioned fail them, they don't have a plan B that'll convince them to get back on their feet and continue striving for success. There have been several times in my life where I could've, would've, and should've just quit and went in another direction. But I've always found it within me to soldier on, taking the blows to come back swinging harder. This is the reason that I continue to strive toward success.

There have been several key moments in my life that I could've thrown in the towel. I remember in the fifth grade, I took a math test, and I got a 60-something on it. One of my classmates shouted out in front of everybody, "Ooo, Lester! You failed the test! How can you ever become a doctor if you fail a math test?" I looked at this knucklehead and said, "This was only one test, and it was obvious I wasn't prepared. But I'll be prepared next time." The next test and the next and the next, I scored between 95 and 100. What would've happened if I took my classmate's critique to heart and quit?

The next significant event was when I was in sixth grade. The teachers were trying to decide whether to move me to seventh grade or hold me back in sixth grade. They promoted me to seventh grade on a trial basis. That summer prior to seventh grade was probably the most productive summer I've ever had. Not that I had much fun that summer because I was mostly relegated to the household due to my indiscretions from the previous year, but instead of acting out even worse, I became very introspective, and I saw all my mistakes and what effect they had on me and my family. They were asking questions I couldn't answer like "How can such a bright person do so many stupid things?" That summer, I told myself I was tired of getting into trouble. I was tired of being punished. I was tired of being grounded and perceived as a troublemaker. And I decided that I was going to put my head down into books and block out all the noise around me. I was determined to prove everybody wrong.

My first gross-anatomy quiz in medical school, I got a 70. One of the gross-anatomy professors seemed to want to help poor minority students, but he did not have much respect for our intelligence. He was often condescending. He walked up to me and said, "Well, Lester. It seems you didn't do very well on that quiz. This doesn't bode well for you in the future. I don't see you moving forward and getting any better if you start out like this." I snapped back, "Well, that's why they call it a drawing board, so I better get back to it!" Everybody heard our exchange and started cracking up laughing. He turned beet red, and with an angry growl, he muttered, "You're incorrigible!" Then he stormed off. It wasn't until he left that it occurred to me that this dude was not in my corner and was never in my corner. He said what he said to try to discourage me.

Needless to say, I completed and passed all my courses within four years, graduated, and went on to become a pediatrician—a goal that I've always wanted to attain since I was five years old—and now, not to boast, I've been noted as one of the three top pediatricians in the city of Atlanta for the past four to five years and hopefully counting. I tell my story to many aspiring physicians, especially ones of color, as often as I can. Determination and hard work are the keys to success and always will be.

CHARLES GOLDEN III

"What's In the Heart of This Black Man"

I HAVE A GREAT since of self-worth, primarily due to the support and love that I received from my family and friends throughout my life. My father, who was the prominent figure, taught me to stand up and face situations as they are and as I wanted them to be. He was strong and always gave me examples of what kind of man he was, but he always told me that I had to find out what kind of man I wanted to be, and whatever decisions I made, I had to be prepared to live with the outcome. But most importantly, he taught me that the world can take away everything but your *word*. That is up to you to give away. I do struggle with ensuring that my children learn the life lessons that I feel they need to succeed today due to ever-increasing single-parent homes and societal climate change. My mother did her best to protect me; as I grew, I came to understand the many sacrifices she had to make to ensure we were loved, fed, and always felt safe. She also helped strengthen and maintain my religious beliefs. She was my rock that sheltered me from the storm, ensuring that I always remain selfless and not hurt anyone purposely. Spending time in the US military also taught me different paradigms of leadership, which helped me understand people's differences based on their life experience.

The legacy that I want to leave not just to my children but to anyone is this: First, find an example of someone that you want to be. Understand how they got where they are in life, but don't just follow them blindly; use their experiences to help you figure it out for yourself. Understand that nothing comes easy, you *will* fail, so do not be afraid; you must fight to succeed. The world is vast, and you must immerse yourself in as much culture as you can. And remember that everyone brings something to the table that you can use to further your goal. Understanding those around you can only strengthen who you are. And always, no matter the circumstances, treat everyone the way you want to be treated.

DR. ERICK HALL SR.

What's in the Heart of This Black Man

THE BLACK MAN'S EXPERIENCE IN AMERICA

IT IS TIME TO change the narrative and perception of the Black man in America. The world is ready for it, and Black men are at the forefront of movements that can move the needle. The Black man's experience in America is one that is filled with both pain and strength. From the pain of hundreds of years of oppression to the strength of overcoming all odds, the Black man has always been a source of inspiration. Despite everything, he has persevered and carved out a place for himself in this country.

Now more than ever, it is important to listen to the Black man's voice. He has a lot to say about what it means to be a Black man in America today. He can provide insight into the issues that matter most to him and his community. He can also offer hope for the future. We can learn more about ourselves and our country by listening to the Black man's story.

THE BLACK MAN'S VIEW OF HIMSELF

A deep sense of pride is in the heart of a Black man in America, even though he has a feeling that there is still something missing deep down in his heart. The void he is feeling is due to the lack of knowing his true identity. He would be even prouder if he knew his true heritage and culture—if it were not stolen on the voyage across the Atlantic from his homeland Africa. Despite all his obstacles, he is proud of his achievements. He is proud of his family and his communities. And yet, he also carries a heavy burden. He knows that he is not truly free in this country, no matter how hard he works or how much success he achieves. He knows that he is still treated as a second-class citizen and that his lives matter less than those of his White counterparts. He is aware of the odds stacked against him. He has to work twice as hard just to get half as far. But he also knows he is strong enough to overcome any challenge.

THE BLACK MAN'S VIEW OF OTHERS

Perhaps no other group of people has been more demonized in the media than Black men.

There are numerous stereotypes and assumptions out there about Black men. They are often portrayed as violent, aggressive, and unemotional. But the reality is that Black men are some of the most loving, compassionate, and tenderhearted people on the planet.

They know how to love with their whole hearts, and they do so with an unmatched intensity.

It is a well-established fact that the Black man has always been viewed as a lesser being in society. This is evident in how they are treated by the police, the workplace, and in their everyday lives. However, the way Black men view themselves is not so well-known. Despite everything, they still have hearts full of love and compassion for others. They can still see the good in people, even when it isn't always reciprocated. This is what makes them such unique individuals.

THE BLACK MAN'S DETERMINATION

It is no secret that the Black man has long been misunderstood and mistreated in America. Even in the twenty-first century, we are still fighting for equality and respect. But through it all, we have persevered. We have overcome incredible odds to become successful in every field, from business to entertainment to politics.

And yet, despite our achievements, we still face racism and discrimination. We are still treated as if we are inferior to other groups. This is why it is so essential for us to tell our own stories in our voices. We need to show the world who we really are.

One of the most essential things for Black men is staying connected to our roots. We must never forget our roots and what we have been through. Only then can we truly appreciate our accomplishments.

It is also important for us to support each other. Too many Black men still buy into the negative stereotypes about us. We need to lift each other and celebrate our successes. We must show the world we are proud of who we are and what we have achieved.

THE BLACK MAN'S LOVE LIFE

Love is the most powerful emotion that a Black man can feel. It is an emotion that can make him do things he never thought possible. Love is what makes a Black man's heartbeat strong. The Black man's love is the most beautiful and powerful thing in the world. It is a force that can overcome any obstacle, and it is something that should be cherished and protected. The Black man's love is something that should be celebrated and honored. It should be taken seriously, and it is something that should be respected.

The Black man is a great lover who has a remarkable ability to adorn women. With her, he's a provider, protector, planner, peacemaker, and prayer warrior.

These attributes that he possesses are unique and inherent. It is believed that God, the creator of humanity, intentionally created man in this form so that he could be the head, and in turn, he will be a husband to the woman. It is, however, safe to say that I believe every woman needs these 5 Ps that a man possesses (provider, protector, peacemaker, planner, and prayer warrior).

The man, as a provider, is naturally saddled with the responsibility to provide for his family's needs. He tries to support his family and find stability regardless of socioeconomic class. These needs could be basic or more complex. He's to protect his family from danger at all costs, and he will create a friendly environment for his family, so he has to shield them from danger; it is often believed that when a male figure is in the home, the chances of getting into trouble are very slim. He is also a man who sees the peaceful coordination of his home.

A common saying is "a family that prays together, stays together." The man is a prayer warrior who stands in the gap for his family and wars in prayers. He's a planner who governs home affairs and helps create plans to help his family achieve their objectives.

It is often said that women are weaker vessels, which would mean that for every woman to live out her life fully, she would need a man with all the forenamed attributes to thrive.

There is a philosophical theory that no man can survive in isolation, human beings are social animals, and they are to interact with each other to achieve their goals. This theory applies to all people. We have people who stay indoors more often than others, yet there is always a need to interact with others. This shows why offenders are sentenced to isolation (prison) to punish them for their crimes. Prison or isolation centers have correctional facilities used to curb immoral vices in humans.

True joy and happiness come from sharing beautiful moments with the ones you love.

THROUGH GOD, WE WILL ALWAYS BE VICTORIOUS

In conclusion, as a Black man, I believe we are resilient people, highly adaptable, and totally indestructible because we were chosen before the foundation of the Earth by Our Creator. We are fully capable of loving all of humanity; we have emotions, and we are brave, smart, intelligent, critical thinkers and problem solvers. Even though we live in a world where fearful and dreadful things surround us, our triumph is this: "greater is he that is in you than he that is in the world." We can trust that God promises we will come out victorious.

REVEREND GARY JACKSON

Fire and Life International Ministries

I WAS RECENTLY ASKED the question, "What's in the heart of this Black man?"

Let me first introduce myself. I am a middle-aged Black man, born and raised in the Northeastern region, and my parents, originally from the Southern region of America, granted me the experience of various cultures of America. A husband of over thirty years, a father of four, a former amateur boxer, an enlisted Air Force disabled veteran, an entrepreneur, and a minister of the gospel of Jesus Christ—that's me.

Along with these life experiences, I must also factor in the mistakes, mishaps, and pitfalls of a defeated mindset that led to homelessness on more than one occasion. To say the least, I have experienced quite a bit over the years; thus, I realize that it is through these experiences that the heart of my worldview, personality, intellect, emotions, and physical being are still developing.

This brings me to a point in my present life, what I identify as an awakening. In 2022, I experienced healing from cancer, near drowning in the Bahamas, and an awakening in Ghana, West Africa.

I am so grateful to celebrate being cancer free! I am humbled and without words for the peace of God that caused me not to panic while struggling for my life in the ocean. I give God praise and glorify Him because He is mightier than cancer and greater than the ocean.

In Ghana, I visited the Cape Coast Castle. This is where millions of enslaved Africans were tortured, raped, sold as property, and shipped to numerous parts of the world by their captors.

I stood in the very dungeons that my ancestors were in chains and shackles. My heart was shattered as I learned how many died in that very dungeon of starvation and disease. All the while, right above this dungeon was the church where the captors praised and worshipped their god.

As I listened to our tour guide go into horrific details about how they were treated, I realized that only the physically and mentally strong survived. I understand that if it were not for this strength, I would not have existence.

I walked where the slaves walked as they were led out of "the door of no return" to ships to be dispersed around the world.

It was then that I understood they would never see their loved ones again; they lost their names, culture, language, and religion.

The Cape Coast Castle experience alone directly impacted my worldview—and my identity—and challenged my faith and purpose in life. In that moment, I was moved emotionally, and I realized that my heart was beginning to harden. There was an older gentleman next to me who was emotionally moved as well. He said to me, "Brother, we can leave here bitter or leave here better." These words started the healing process of bringing a fragmented heart into a whole.

I must conclude by saying that out of every *mountaintop* and *valley low* experience, all that God has allowed me to go through has humbled my heart, transformed my heart, and made my heart stronger. I come to know that God's purpose for me in life is greater than me. God is truly in control, and I can trust Him with my whole heart. I look forward to taking these experiences, sharing my heart, and impacting the world to bring change.

CLEMENT JOHNSON

What's in the Heart of This Black Man

MY UPBRINGING CONTRIBUTED TO the man I am today. I was born in Newark, New Jersey, but I have no memory of the city or my relatives. My mom and father did not last, so mom moved to Oklahoma City with my stepfather when I was three years old.

This framed my understanding that being alone is okay, and setting your direction and listening to older people's advice is a good thing. My early memories were of a small family without a support system. I was pretty much in a place my family wasn't; we didn't know anybody. At a young age, I learned to care for myself since I didn't have that family structure; I would care for myself and my older sister. I was six.

Later in the year, Mom moved to Los Angeles, where life continued to be difficult. When I was eight, my stepfather was shot in our apartment building and spent the rest of his life paralyzed from the waist down. I had healthcare responsibilities for my stepfather, which kept me even more isolated. This formed my character of understanding things take time and the trait of surviving through pain. Seeing my stepfather recover took years of medical care no kid should have to administer, but it formed this Black man.

We moved to Compton, California, when I was in junior high school. Living in the gang-ridden area of Los Angeles proved that when people are downgraded by society, the result is backlash. Rarely did someone show interest in me or any of our community to help us grow. I never saw Black businesses flourish. I never met a Black business owner until I was in the Marine Corps. The streets of Compton were separated. Gangs separated neighborhoods, race separated friends, and people of knowledge didn't reach out beyond the boundary.

The legacy I would like to leave to future generations is this: literacy and education matter. Sharing time with our Black youth is important. It takes patience to cultivate tidbits of time to influence a person through mentorship and example. Through my business, I hope to assist young Black men and women in the career field of technology. I will use the tools of mentorship, courseware, certifications, and job placement to put this plan into action.

My influences come from my upbringing in the Black community. The Black community taught me that life is hard and the decisions you make today affect the course of your life. I joined the Marines at nineteen and retired after serving twenty-four years. The Marines cultivated my view of other races and opened a window to meet rural people. The Marines also introduced me to the world, where I met people from other countries with cultures highly focused on family. It influenced my ability to plan and make hard and unpopular decisions in leadership and life.

This influence carried over into my pursuing education, where I received two bachelor's and two master's degrees, and I currently own two businesses. This demonstrates literacy, regardless of your socioeconomic status, and with a little fortitude, educational achievements are possible.

I have been married to my lovely wife for thirty-seven years. She has made me a better person and focused me on the community and our Black youth. Being married as long as we have always grabs the attention of Black youth and gives instant credibility while highlighting stability.

DR. MUTEBA MUKENDI

What's in the Heart of This Black Man

AS A SECOND-GENERATION AMERICAN, I've always carried the hopes and dreams of my predecessors near my heart. The dreams of prosperity, for the nation, for the family, and for self.   I stand firmly on the shoulders of parents who willed themselves toward a better future for their offspring, a journey that began when my father was offered an opportunity to study in the US after being awarded a Fulbright scholarship. Without much money at hand and very little English, they started their new lives.

I was born in Athens, Ohio. When my dad completed his studies, we moved to Pennsylvania, where he undertook a doctoral program. Pittsburgh was what I called home for a while. It was the only home I knew. I was a quiet kid but inquisitive. I knew I was much more than another Black boy with a so-called funny name. I knew I hadn't felt the sense of belonging that typically comes with having a solid family unit or living in a decent community. Instead, I felt like an outsider.

Years later, we left the US to pursue what would become a six-year journey through several countries in Africa. My dad's job with the United Nations was his opportunity to return and contribute to the advancement of African nations. For me, it was more daunting. Before moving, I grew up not truly understanding or appreciating the many identities I hold, being a Congolese American, bilingual, bicultured, young Black lad. It wasn't until we crossed the Atlantic Ocean that I was forced to reckon with my identities.

For the first time, I was able to see others who looked like me, with names just as distinguishing as mine. I also saw people who lived in lack but still found joy. Kids made makeshift toys, families shared the little they had, and people gathered together and forgot all the cares in the world. I was in awe that even in the face of war and calamity, people found solace in each other. There was something about the culture that intrigued me. This shared learning taught me values that hold true to this day. I learned what true generosity means, how family comes first, and how to be forever grateful to God for the many blessings He's bestowed on His people.

When we returned to the US, I stayed true to these cultural values. In the face of storms, I held true to the peace that steadies my figurative ship. The Black man I am today is a result of my lived experiences and those that I witnessed during my travels. I am now assured of who I am because of what inheritance I received. My inheritance was never in the richness of the African land but rather in the depth of the African culture. In my opinion, being a Black man in this day and age can be distressing and demoralizing, placing even greater importance on having a clear vision and purpose. My hope is for future generations of Black men to build an appreciation for our ancestral culture. As such, I aim to inspire others to develop communities where a sense of belonging can be cultivated.

TROY L. RAWLINGS

What's in the Heart of This Black Man

CLEAR AND PRESENT

AS I RUBBED MY father's head to soothe his aching breaths, I thought back to the most profound thing I ever remember him saying to me in my whole life. "I really didn't have any plans after high school," answered my dad after I asked him what his goals were after high school.

This seemed like a pretty basic question, since most teachers asked it at the beginning of the year. Dad's answer shocked me. A star athlete in high school, who lettered in football and baseball, and an amazing fine artist with a great sense of humor, he was such a talented and brilliant young man. It was even rumored that Major League Baseball scouts were looking at him, to which my dad replied, "They weren't looking at young Black players back then."

Back then meant 1963 or so. His answer also shocked me because I don't ever remember not having a plan for my life or goals I wished to achieve.

Three months earlier, my father had been diagnosed with acute leukemia.

From what I know now, it's a very aggressive form of leukemia. But even if it wasn't, between the drugs and alcohol use, bad eating habits, depression, and overall poor health practices, disease was bound to win this battle against my dad. Now, laying at home in his bed, just a frail shell of his former self, my father struggled to try to speak but couldn't get the words out. He literally didn't have enough strength to talk. So, I spoke.

"Well done. It's okay. Rest now. Thank you. I love you." These were some of the loving, caring, compassionate words I wanted him to hear. Though my father lived and fought with depression, he would always spread joy, grace, and kindness to others. I embody that legacy of being a joy-giver. Coming up the way I did makes me, for better or worse, who I am today. Striving to be the best father possible to my daughter comes from not only knowing abandonment as a teenager but having and choosing amazing fathers and father figures to be friends and mentors in my life.

Today, I continually love me. That means celebrating my wins, setting goals and striving to achieve them, loving others and God unconditionally, and learning to be and practicing being a man of my word. Being *clear* and transparent enough for someone to look at me and see their reflection, like in a still stream, and *present* enough to build trust and security in my daughter and others who depend or will depend on me in the future. I desire to leave a legacy of love, understanding, enrichment, and tangible equity that will secure future generations. But this all starts by waking up daily and committing to doing the things I am gifted at. Our gifts beget gifts. Our fire sparks and ignites the fire in others. I will be present every day.

LACEY "G SOULDIER" TURNER

What's in the Heart of This Black Man?

AS I SIT HERE and ponder that question, I reflect on my life as a child up until now. What's in my heart is pain, confusion, happiness, pride, sadness, delight, and anger. You might say, "Lacey, how can you feel all these different emotions in your heart?" It's quite simple. The answer to that question is because I'm a Black man. I feel pain because of the trauma I see constantly in the Black communities. Pain from the undiagnosed mental illnesses that cause people to suffer, do drugs, or commit violent crimes against each other. At times, I feel guilty for being highly successful with the things that I'm achieving in life as I see homelessness and other Black people struggling to make it out of poverty. I feel confused and angry because I don't understand how cops can gun a Black man down because of the color of their skin. I, myself, have been verbally abused and harassed by police officers for no apparent reason. This abuse has happened from my childhood to adulthood. I feel pain on the inside because when I was a little kid, I had dreams of becoming a police officer when they used to come to our schools and speak. Now, years later, I see those same officers gunning down people I know.

I feel proud because I take pride in being Black. Some look at their Black skin as a curse. I'm proud to be part of a powerful, prominent culture. I love the way we Black people dress, and I love our music, food, and family traditions. I'm proud because I was able to make something out of nothing in a system that is designed for the Black man to fail. I overcame each and every obstacle that was meant to hold me back. I lifted every boulder off my shoulders that tried to break my spirit and make me quit. I feel delight because I have accomplished so much in my life;

I've been a tutor, a mentor serving with AmeriCorps, an award-winning film writer and director, a hip-hop artist, a published author, an activist, a journalist, an actor, a podcaster, and a business owner. I'm humble, yet I am a king. As a Black man, I am powerful beyond measure. I don't subscribe to the labels of low paradigms that America has tried to place on me.

I'm happy to come from a lineage of people who went through horrific circumstances that were meant to break their spirit, only for them to rise through the carnage and ashes and fight for the freedoms that we have today. Many of our ancestors lost their lives to create change. That same courage that our ancestors had lives through my heart. I am brave and not afraid to die for what I believe in. And last but not least, I feel sad because we have yet to break this monotony in this democracy that's a mockery full of hypocrisy. What's in the heart of this Black man is that I am the master of my own mind. I have reached a level of total supremacy that no one and nothing can ever take from me. I have my black belt in being a Black man.

CURTIS J. YOUNG

Edited by Monarch Young

What's in the Heart of This Black Man?

I, CURTIS J. YOUNG, was born on December 15, 1981, as the eldest of multiple siblings on both my mom and dad's side of the family. Growing up, I often explored my creative purpose in life but was often swayed by the opinion of others telling me who I was to become. I was very timid and lacked the confidence to voice my opinion. There were times I just agreed to conform in fear of speaking up for myself about what was truly in my heart.

I was a young, lost soul without a clue where life would take me. I moved seventeen times before the age of eighteen and missed key curriculum components vital for literacy development. Racial tension was brewing in the community, and I wanted to break free from the violence within my home and surrounding cities. These experiences in life escalated my frustration and diminished any hope of amounting to greatness. My heart began to grow cold.

A pivotal turning point occurred in my life at the tender age of eleven while trying to break up a domestic argument between my parents. I built up the courage to confront my dad and told him to ease up. He responded in rage that he was not my father and, against my mother's will, revealed to me that my real dad was Dr. Dre. I was in shock and absolutely dumbfounded. At that moment, my whole world was in disarray, and my heart sunk.

Football was my outlet for aggression, but due to a race-related altercation, I was sentenced to juvenile detention and ineligible to ever step out on the field again. Music became my escape. Throughout the next decade, I began to feel a void in my life and desired to meet my dad. In 2001, at the age of twenty,

I would finally get the chance to meet my father figure, Andre Romelle Young, a.k.a. Dr. Dre. I wanted to be iconic just like him, mirror his vocal imprint, and embody his persona. Through idolizing him and wanting to walk in his shoes, my heart moved farther away from finding my true identity and who I was destined to be.

Five years later, I would meet my life partner, Monarch, off Sunset Blvd in Hollywood, California. Being in her presence made my heart skip a beat. I was intrigued by her brains, beauty, grace, and confidence. She supported my passion for music, and I was infatuated by her adoration of me. Over time, I became influenced by the ways of the world and the enemy's deception. My conduct would eventually lead us down a road of betrayal and destruction. We married in our brokenness, which brought fuel to the fire as history began to repeat. I began to lyrically pour my pain and poison onto tracks for profit. Pride began to grow in my soul at the very taste of stardom, which would eventually become my downfall. I was stripped of everything, fell flat on my face, and my heart was humbled.

I called out to the Creator of life at my weakest moment, sought wisdom from the Word, and overcame the toxic patterns of my past. My eyes were enlightened to truth and the powerful weapon of the tongue. I started speaking life into lyrics as a vocal vessel and using the rooted gift within my DNA in fulfillment of purpose. My heart no longer desired to roll down death row but instead wanted to walk the narrow path of this newfound freedom. I am honored to create a monarchy of artistry that redefines the beat of a global music culture and inspires the human race to embrace their royalty.

CONCLUSION

IN MY WRITING OF this book, my goals were to explain my true feelings of what's in the heart of this Black man. Since I couldn't speak for us all, I wrote this book. I believe mind, body, and soul are three equal pieces that make a person complete when understanding a Black man's point of view. Everyone has a different path, and what shaped their thought process, their visions, and who they are today goes back to birth in what was always taught to them growing up. Many of the things taught to us come from the previous generation, and we must learn from those who came before us. Many times, I do not believe change is factored into their beliefs. The thought of change has not been taught to us because this is the way we have always done things.

As we grow technologically, our worldview must adjust to the changes. Otherwise, we will always be living in the past.

We must be able to adjust to generational changes, but in order to adjust, we must understand that everything we *were* taught may not be how we live our life *currently* or in the *future*. I am not saying that we forget about our upbringing or past family generations, but to be successful, our mindset must focus on current situations and circumstances.

What's in the heart of a Black man depends on him understanding past generations and changing situations and circumstances. Life is a series of circles, cycles, phrases, and stages—our experiences that teach us the lessons of life. We can either ignore them or *embrace* change, but it requires understanding that we might have to make difficult changes to adjust to what is truly in our heart. If we hold or repeat the past, it is never going to change.

I can truly tell you that I had to embrace change, and I had to embrace the formula for change. There are two:

- Current hehavior + vision = change

- Current behavior + intolerable pain = change

The world is always changing; we can adjust, or we can stay where we are, but change is inevitable. We can learn with the brain, or we can learn with the pain. In my heart, I have learned to adjust to change. I still remember the many things that happened when I was a child and what my aunts, my uncle, and my grandmother instilled in me. That was what they knew to be true at the time. As I grew, I had to figure out through my experiences, trials, tribulations, failures, and getting knocked down by our Lord and Savior many times that you have to see things not as they are, not as they were taught to you, but how they should be. Therefore, in writing this book, I hope that I was able to convey to my readers exactly what I learned and what I believe to be in my heart.

There were a few things that I learned that shaped my thought process today. The most important thing was to not live in the past. Our focus should be on how we live life today, but I believe our vision should be what we can do to make life better tomorrow. I call this *vision, understanding, and focus theory* (VUF). This provides a roadmap for not always looking backward to what happened in previous generations or being bitter that we have to get revenge, but choosing to live in the now.

It provides focus on what will be our legacy in preparing our future generations to tackle today's challenges to solve tomorrow's potential issues.

Another revelation that I learned in writing this book was that we must set goals to be successful; just the act of setting goals does not achieve goals. It requires a plan, and I came up with what I call *motivation, determination, and creation theory* (MDC). Once a person truly realizes what they want to do, they have to be motivated to do it. Motivation requires a person to understand their reason for the goals they set for themselves. To achieve goals, it requires a strong sense of determination. Determination means whatever is required must get done—with effort, hard work, and most importantly, heart. Creation is achieving goals based on our vision and seeing a final product, which gives us a great sense of accomplishment.

This leads us to what's in the heart of this Black man. I believe we must be willing to let go of the past and break away from generational curses. We must be able to recognize that we are not in the same time period as yesterday, and we have to focus on today to be able to move forward and prepare for tomorrow. I believe in the words of Dr. Martin Luther King Jr. that we must learn to live together, work together, and talk together, as stated in his "I Had a Dream" speech. It is my interpretation that, in his dreams, he saw things not as they *were* but as they should *be*.

I encourage my readers to remember the past but not live it. Live today and formulate dreams for a better tomorrow. This is what is truly in the heart of this Black man: love, compassion, honesty, integrity, and ethics. Let us all live by these core values to make the world a better place.

Thank you.

ACKNOWLEDGMENTS

FIRST AND FOREMOST, I have to thank my Lord and Savior Jesus Christ for maintaining his faith in me that I would do his work. I must thank John Koehler, my publisher, who believed in my vision and gave me an opportunity to tell it. I would also like to thank Dr. Telishia Berry for inviting me to be a coauthor in her book *The Heart of a Black Man*. Her idea propelled me to write this book. I would like to thank Dr. Michael Mantell for his constant encouragement and guidance that kept me inspired and Dr. Erick Hall Sr. for his confidence and courage that helped keep me motivated to be the best person that I can be.

I want to acknowledge my grandmother (Mattie Blake Stephens) who was my inspiration and still is the reason why I am the man I am today. I must acknowledge my mother (Gladys Stephens) for always being there for me and seeing that I had to get away from the current environment that I was in. I still don't understand why she chose my brother Jerry and me (out of her ten children). I am so grateful to be lucky-number seven in the chain of her children. Check out my previous book *Country Boy, City Boy: A Journey That Ain't Over Yet* for more about that.

I owe a debt of gratitude to my four children (James III, DeAngelo, Brittany, and Joshua), who still do not understand why Dad is the way he is today and why my thought process and focus have always been about honesty, integrity, and ethics. We should not worry about what others think about us if we are truly committed to being ourselves.

Most importantly, I must thank my exceptionally beautiful wife and soulmate, Dr. Michelle Denise Cooley. The seventeen years of knowing and being with her helped truly shape me into the person I am today. I could not have achieved success without her. My successes are her successes. When my mind could not visualize something just yet, her conversation, wisdom, understanding, and focus helped get me there. I love you, baby.

In conclusion, I must acknowledge all the people who have come into my life and shown me that life is full of circles, cycles, phases, and stages. You can either accept and embrace them or ignore them. These are the things that shape our thoughts and visions about our path.

These things are what shape my vision, understanding, and focus, and sharing them is why I wrote *A Black Man's Point of View—Mind, Body, and Soul.*

Thank you so much, dear readers, for reading.